interchange

FIFTH EDITION

2A

Workbook

Jack C. Richards
with Jonathan Hull and Susan Proctor

CAMBRIDGE
UNIVERSITY PRESS

CAMBRIDGE
UNIVERSITY PRESS

University Printing House, Cambridge CB2 8BS, United Kingdom

One Liberty Plaza, 20th Floor, New York, NY 10006, USA

477 Williamstown Road, Port Melbourne, VIC 3207, Australia

4843/24, 2nd Floor, Ansari Road, Daryaganj, Delhi – 110002, India

79 Anson Road, #06–04/06, Singapore 079906

Cambridge University Press is part of the University of Cambridge.

It furthers the University's mission by disseminating knowledge in the pursuit of
education, learning and research at the highest international levels of excellence.

www.cambridge.org
Information on this title: www.cambridge.org/9781316622704

First published 1998
Second edition 2005
Third edition 2013
20 19 18 17 16 15 14 13 12 11 10 9 8 7 6 5 4 3 2 1

Printed in Malaysia by Vivar Printing

A catalogue record for this publication is available from the British Library.

ISBN	9781316620236	Student's Book 2 with Online Self-Study
ISBN	9781316620250	Student's Book 2A with Online Self-Study
ISBN	9781316620328	Student's Book 2B with Online Self-Study
ISBN	9781316620342	Student's Book 2 with Online Self-Study and Online Workbook
ISBN	9781316620366	Student's Book 2A with Online Self-Study and Online Workbook
ISBN	9781316620373	Student's Book 2B with Online Self-Study and Online Workbook
ISBN	9781316622698	Workbook 2
ISBN	9781316622704	Workbook 2A
ISBN	9781316622711	Workbook 2B
ISBN	9781316622728	Teacher's Edition 2 with Complete Assessment Program
ISBN	9781316622285	Class Audio 2 CDs
ISBN	9781316623992	Full Contact 2 with Online Self-Study
ISBN	9781316624005	Full Contact 2A with Online Self-Study
ISBN	9781316624029	Full Contact 2B with Online Self-Study
ISBN	9781316622254	Presentation Plus 2

Additional resources for this publication at www.cambridge.org/interchange

Contents

	Credits	iv
1	Good memories	1
2	Life in the city	7
3	Making changes	13
4	Have you ever tried it?	19
5	Hit the road!	25
6	Sure! I'll do it.	31
7	What do you use this for?	37
8	Time to celebrate!	43

Credits

Illustrations

337 Jon (KJA Artists): 4, 22; **417 Neal** (KJA Artists): 1, 16, 67, 84, 90; **Mark Duffin** (Victrola, telephone): 39, 51; **Thomas Girard** (Good Illustration): 32, 87; **John Goodwin** (Eye Candy Illustration): 36, 94; **Gary Venn** (Lemonade Illustration Agency): 30, 64; **Quino Marin** (The Organisation): 79, 91; **Gavin Reece** (New Division): 85; **Paul Williams** (Sylvie Poggio Artists): 42.

Photos

Back cover (woman with whiteboard): Jenny Acheson/Stockbyte/GettyImages; Back cover (whiteboard): Nemida/GettyImages; Back cover (man using phone): Betsie Van Der Meer/Taxi/GettyImages; Back cover (woman smiling): PeopleImages.com/DigitalVision/GettyImages; Back cover (name tag): Tetra Images/GettyImages; Back cover (handshake): David Lees/Taxi/GettyImages; p. 2: JackF/iStock/Getty Images Plus/GettyImages; p. 3: Slaven Vlasic/Getty Images Entertainment/GettyImages; p. 5: Baar/ullstein bild/GettyImages; p. 6: Jetta Productions/Stone/GettyImages; p. 7 (TL): Vasilii Kosarev/EyeEm/GettyImages; p. 7 (TR): skynesher/E+/GettyImages; p. 7 (CL): Richard Newstead/Moment/GettyImages; p. 7 (CR): Scott Olson/Getty Images News/GettyImages; p. 7 (BL): Cultura RM Exclusive/Dan Dunkley/Cultura Exclusive/GettyImages; p. 7 (BR): ALAN SCHEIN/GettyImages; p. 8: Daniel Allan/Photodisc/GettyImages; p. 10 (cable railway): Anthony Collins/Photodisc/GettyImages; p. 10 (ferry): Michael Coyne/Lonely Planet Images/GettyImages; p. 10 (subway): GILLARDI Jacques/hemis.fr/GettyImages; p. 10 (tram): marco wong/Moment/GettyImages; p. 11: Jack Hollingsworth/Stockbyte/GettyImages; p. 12: Sven Hagolani/GettyImages; p. 13: Stewart Cohen/The Image Bank/GettyImages; p. 14 (CR): H. Armstrong Roberts/ClassicStock/Archive Photos/GettyImages; p. 14 (BR): Johner Images/Brand X Pictures/GettyImages; p. 17: Jake Fitzjones/Dorling Kindersley/GettyImages; p. 18 (TR): Goodluz/iStock/Getty Images Plus/GettyImages; p. 18 (CL): KingWu/iStock/Getty Images Plus/GettyImages; p. 18 (BR): Coprid/iStock/Getty Images Plus/GettyImages; p. 19: Ethan Daniels/WaterFrame/GettyImages; p. 20: Thinkstock/Stockbyte/GettyImages; p. 21 (BL): 4FR/iStock/Getty Images Plus/GettyImages; p. 21 (T): Bolot/E+/GettyImages; p. 21 (BR): Lise Metzger/The Image Bank/GettyImages; p. 22: Lartal/Photolibrary/GettyImages; p. 23: Tony Robins/Photolibrary/GettyImages; p. 24 (CR): Anthony Lee/OJO Images/GettyImages; p. 24 (BR): Steve Brown Photography/Photolibrary/GettyImages; p. 25: Xavier Arnau/Vetta/GettyImages; p. 27 (C): Leonardo Martins/Moment/GettyImages; p. 27 (T): Michele Falzone/AWL Images/GettyImages; p. 27 (B): Michele Falzone/AWL Images/GettyImages; p. 28: FRED DUFOUR/AFP/GettyImages; p. 29: Hero Images/GettyImages; p. 30 (L): Tomasz Konczuk/EyeEm/GettyImages; p. 30 (R): OcusFocus/iStock/Getty Images Plus/GettyImages; p. 31: John Howard/DigitalVision/GettyImages; p. 33 (R): Blend Images-KidStock/Brand X Pictures/GettyImages; p. 33 (L): Laoshi/E+/GettyImages; p. 34: Rich Legg/E+/GettyImages; p. 35: DreamPictures/Blend Images/GettyImages; p. 37 (Ex 1.2): altrendo images/GettyImages; p. 37 (Ex 1.2): Maximilian Stock Ltd./Oxford Scientific/GettyImages; p. 37 (Ex 1.3): Tony Cordoza/Photographer's Choice/GettyImages; p. 37 (Ex 1.4): Tetra Images/GettyImages; p. 37 (Ex 1.5): Peter Dazeley/Photographer's Choice/GettyImages; p. 38: VCG/Visual China Group/GettyImages; p. 39 (TL): Stock Montage/GettyImages; p. 39 (TR): Roberto Machado Noa/LightRocket/GettyImages; p. 39 (CR): Ivan Stevanovic/E+/GettyImages; p. 39 (BR): Justin Sullivan/Getty Images News/GettyImages; p. 41 (Ex 8.1): Westend61/GettyImages; p. 41 (Ex 8.2): Prykhodov/iStock/Getty Images Plus/GettyImages; p. 41 (Ex 8.3): Jeffrey Hamilton/Stockbyte/GettyImages; p. 41 (Ex 8.4): Paul Bradbury/Caiaimage/GettyImages; p. 41 (Ex 8.5): sputnikos/iStock/Getty Images Plus/GettyImages; p. 41 (Ex 8.6): Image Source/GettyImages; p. 43 (TR): Charles Ommanney/The Washington Post/GettyImages; p. 43 (BR): Tetra Images/GettyImages; p. 44 (Ex 1.2): altrendo images/GettyImages; p. 45 (Martin Luther): FPG/Hulton Archive/GettyImages; p. 45 (Valentine's Day): Dorling Kindersley/GettyImages; p. 45 (April Fools' Day): Wodicka/ullstein bild/GettyImages; p. 45 (Mother's Day): Ariel Skelley/Blend Images/GettyImages; p. 45 (Father's Day): Ariel Skelley/Blend Images/GettyImages; p. 45 (Independence Day): Tetra Images/GettyImages; p. 45 (Labor Day): Blend Images-Ronnie Kaufman/Larry Hirshowitz/Brand X Pictures/GettyImages; p. 45 (Thanksgiving): Paul Poplis/Photolibrary/GettyImages; p. 46 (TR): PeopleImages/DigitalVision/GettyImages; p. 46 (CR): Floresco Productions/OJO Images/GettyImages; p. 47 (Japan): Eriko Koga/Taxi Japan/GettyImages; p. 47 (Morocco): Hisham Ibrahim/Photographer's Choice/GettyImages; p. 47 (Scotland): Education Images/Universal Images Group/GettyImages; p. 47 (India): Jihan Abdalla/Blend Images/GettyImages; p. 48: RubberBall Productions/Brand X Pictures/GettyImages; p. 49: Dan Dalton/Caiaimage/GettyImages; p. 50 (Ex 3.1 photo 1): JTB Photo/Universal Images Group/GettyImages; p. 50 (Ex 3.1 photo 2): fST Images - Caspar Benson/Brand X Pictures/GettyImages; p. 50 (Ex 3.2 photo 1): Glow Images/GettyImages; p. 50 (Ex 3.2 photo 2): Jason Homa/Blend Images/GettyImages; p. 50 (Ex 3.3 photo 1): David Caudery/PC Format Magazine/GettyImages; p. 50 (Ex 3.3 photo 2): David Caudery/Apple Bookazine/GettyImages; p. 50 (Ex 3.4 photo 1): H. Armstrong Roberts/ClassicStock/GettyImages; p. 50 (Ex 3.4 photo 2): Sydney Roberts/DigitalVision/GettyImages; p. 50 (Ex 3.5 photo 1): Thomas Trutschel/Photothek/GettyImages; p. 50 (Ex 3.5 photo 2): Justin Sullivan/Getty Images News/GettyImages; p. 52: Westend61/GettyImages; p. 54: H. Armstrong Roberts/ClassicStock/Archive Photos/GettyImages; p. 55: JGI/Jamie Grill/Blend Images/GettyImages; p. 58 (Ex 7.1): Roberto Westbrook/Blend Images/GettyImages; p. 58 (Ex 7.2): Marc Romanelli/Blend Images/GettyImages; p. 58 (Ex 7.3): PeopleImages.com/DigitalVision/GettyImages; p. 58 (Ex 7.4): Rick Gomez/Blend Images/GettyImages; p. 58 (Ex 7.5): Ezra Bailey/Taxi/GettyImages; p. 59 (TR): Sam Diephuis/Blend Images/GettyImages; p. 59 (CR): Betsie Van Der Meer/Taxi/GettyImages; p. 60: JGI/Jamie Grill/Blend Images/GettyImages; p. 61: Arcaid/Universal Images Group/GettyImages; p. 62 (Ex 3.1): Matteo Colombo/Moment/GettyImages; p. 62 (Ex 3.2): Alan Copson/Photographer's Choice/GettyImages; p. 62 (Ex 3.3): John Lawson, Belhaven/Moment/GettyImages; p. 62 (Ex 3.4): Lily Chou/Moment/GettyImages; p. 62 (Ex 3.5): De Agostini/W. Buss/De Agostini Picture Library/GettyImages; p. 62 (Ex 3.6): Avatarmin/Moment/GettyImages; p. 63 (CR): Oliver J Davis Photography/Moment/GettyImages; p. 63 (TR): kimrawicz/iStock/Getty Images Plus/GettyImages; p. 64: John Elk III/Lonely Planet Images/GettyImages; p. 65 (C): Christian Adams/Photographer's Choice/GettyImages; p. 65 (BR): Erika Satta/EyeEm/GettyImages; p. 66: Yongyuan Dai/Moment/GettyImages; p. 68 (Ex 4.1): Redrockschool/E+/GettyImages; p. 68 (Ex 4.2): Milenko Bokan/iStock/Getty Images Plus/GettyImages; p. 68 (Ex 4.3): Jetta Productions/Iconica/GettyImages; p. 68 (Ex 4.4): Deklofenak/iStock/Getty Images Plus/GettyImages; p. 69: Rick Diamond/WireImage/GettyImages; p. 70: Marc Romanelli/Blend Images/GettyImages; p. 71: PeopleImages/DigitalVision/GettyImages; p. 72: Jamie Grill/The Image Bank/GettyImages; p. 73: Kris Connor/Getty Images Entertainment/GettyImages; p. 74 (TL): Monica Schipper/FilmMagic/GettyImages; p. 74 (BR): fotoMonkee/E+/GettyImages; p. 75 (TR): Popperfoto/Moviepix/GettyImages; p. 75 (BR): Metro-Goldwyn-Mayer/Archive Photos/GettyImages; p. 76: Buyenlarge/Archive Photos/GettyImages; p. 77: Ernst Haas/Ernst Haas/GettyImages; p. 78: Â©Lions Gate/Courtesy Everett Co/REX/Shutterstock; p. 80: Alan Copson/AWL Images/GettyImages; p. 82: Karl Johaentges/LOOK-foto/Look/GettyImages; p. 83 (T): YinYang/E+/GettyImages; p. 83 (Ex 7.1): Marcio Silva/iStock/Getty Images Plus/GettyImages; p. 83 (Ex 7.2): Gary D'Ercole/Stockbyte/GettyImages; p. 83 (Ex 7.3): Illiano/iStock/Getty Images Plus/GettyImages; p. 83 (Ex 7.4): Silvrshootr/iStock/Getty Images Plus/GettyImages; p. 83 (Ex 7.5): Danita Delimont/Gallo Images/GettyImages; p. 86: BrianAJackson/iStock/Getty Images Plus/GettyImages; p. 88: Monkey Business Images/Monkey Business/Getty Images Plus/GettyImages; p. 92: Sam Edwards/OJO Images/GettyImages; p. 93 (TL), p. 93 (BR): Simon Winnall/Iconica/GettyImages; p. 95: BananaStock/Getty Images Plus/GettyImages; p. 96: Sporrer/Rupp/Cultura/GettyImages.

1 Good memories

1 Past tense

A Write the past tense of these verbs.

Verb	Past tense	Verb	Past tense
be	was/were	hide	
become		laugh	
do		lose	
email		move	
get		open	
have		scream	

B Complete this paragraph. Use the past tense of each of the verbs in part A.

My best friend in school _____was_____ Michael. He and
I _____ in Mrs. Gilbert's third-grade class, and
we _____ friends. We often _____
crazy things in class, but I don't think Mrs. Gilbert ever
really _____ mad at us. For example, Michael
_____ a pet lizard named Peanut. Sometimes he
_____ it in Mrs. Gilbert's desk drawer. Later, when
she _____ the drawer, she always _____
loudly, and the class _____. After two years,
Michael's family _____ to another town. We
_____ each other for a few years, but then we
_____ contact. I often wonder what he's doing now.

2 Complete the questions in this conversation.

Sarah: Welcome to the building. My name's Sarah Walker.

Benedito: Hello. I'm Benedito Peres. It's nice to meet you.

Sarah: Nice to meet you, too. Are you from around here?

Benedito: No, I'm from Brazil.

Sarah: Oh, really? _Were you born_ in Brazil?

Benedito: No, I wasn't born there, actually. I'm originally from Portugal.

Sarah: That's interesting. So, when _____ to Brazil?

Benedito: I moved to Brazil when I was in elementary school.

Sarah: Where _____?

Benedito: We lived in Recife. It's a beautiful city in northeast Brazil. Then I went to college.

Sarah: _____ to school in Recife?

Benedito: No, I went to school in São Paulo.

Sarah: And what _____?

Benedito: Oh, I studied engineering. But I'm here to go to graduate school.

Sarah: Great! When _____?

Benedito: I arrived last week. I start school in three days.

Sarah: Well, good luck. And sorry for all the questions!

3 Answer these questions.

1. Where were you born?

_____

2. Did your family move when you were a child?

_____

3. Did you have a favorite teacher in elementary school?

_____

4. What hobbies did you have when you were a kid?

_____

5. When did you begin to study English?

_____

4 Gael García Bernal

A Scan the article about Gael García Bernal. Where is he from? What does he do?

Gael García Bernal was born in 1978 in Guadalajara, Mexico. As a child, he began to act, and when he was a teenager, he became a star in television soap operas. He decided to go to London to study acting when he was 19. While he was in London, Mexican director Alejandro González Iñárritu invited him to act in the film *Amores Perros*. When it was released in 2000, *Amores Perros* immediately made Gael García Bernal known to the world.

Gael later made many other successful films. With the Mexican actor Diego Luna, he co-starred in *Y tu mamá también* in 2001, a film about two upper-class Mexican teenagers. In 2002, he won the Ariel, Mexico's most important film award, for *El Crimen del Padre Amaro*, the story of a young priest in a small town. Two years later, he worked with the Brazilian director Walter Salles on *The Motorcycle Diaries*, the story of a young Ernesto "Che" Guevara's journey by motorcycle through South America. That same year, Gael worked with the Spanish director Pedro Almodóvar on *Bad Education*. In 2007, Gael directed his first film, *Déficit*, which was about people at a weekend party in Mexico.

As you can see, Gael García Bernal is an international star who works on films in different languages. One of Gael's more recent projects is *Mozart in the Jungle*, an American TV show mostly in English. Gael won a Golden Globe Award in 2016 for playing the lead role, the talented conductor Rodrigo.

Despite his busy career, Gael spends as much time as possible with his son Lázaro and his daughter Libertad. He also likes to sing and make music when he is not acting.

B Check (✓) True or False. For statements that are false, write the correct information.

	True	False
1. Gael García Bernal studied acting in Paris.	☐	☐
2. A Brazilian director directed the film that made him famous.	☐	☐
3. He won an award for his role in *El Crimen del Padre Amaro*.	☐	☐
4. He has never directed a film.	☐	☐
5. He plays a singer in *Mozart in the Jungle*.	☐	☐
6. Gael prefers not to work in foreign language films.	☐	☐

5 Choose the correct word or phrase.

1. I used to collect _____*comic books*_____ (hobbies / scrapbooks / comic books) when I was a kid.

2. My favorite _____ (pet / hobby / place) was a cat called Felix.

3. We used to go to _____ (the playground / summer camp / school) for two weeks during our summer vacations. It was really fun.

4. There was a great _____ (amusement park / playground / beach) on my street. We used to go there every afternoon to play.

6 Look at these childhood pictures of Allie and her brother Robert. Complete the sentences using *used to*.

1. In the summer, Allie and Robert sometimes __*used to go to summer camp*__.

2. They also _____.
Their dog Bruno always used to follow them.

3. Allie _____ every weekend during summer vacation. She hardly ever goes now.

4. Robert _____.
Now they're worth a lot of money.

5. They _____.
They don't have any pets now.

7 Look at the answers. Write the questions using *used to*.

1. **A:** What did you use to do in the summer?

   B: We used to go to the beach.

2. **A:** _____

   B: No, we didn't collect shells. We used to build sand castles.

3. **A:** _____

   B: Yes, we did. We used to swim for hours. Then we played all kinds of sports.

4. **A:** Really? What _____

   B: Well, we used to play beach volleyball with some other kids.

5. **A:** _____

   B: No, we didn't. We used to win!

8 How have you changed in the last five years? Write answers to these questions.

1. What hobbies did you use to have five years ago?

   What hobbies do you have now?

   I used to . . .

   Now, . . .

2. What kind of music did you use to like then?

   What kind of music do you like now?

   _____

   _____

3. What kinds of clothes did you use to like to wear?

   What kinds of clothes do you like to wear now?

   _____

   _____

9 Complete the sentences. Use the past tense of the verbs given.

Paola: I'm an immigrant here. I _____was_____ (be) born in Chile and _____ (grow up) there. I _____ (come) here in 2011. I _____ (not be) very happy at first. Things _____ (be) difficult for me. I _____ (not speak) English, so I _____ (go) to a community college and _____ (study) English there. My English _____ (get) better, and I _____ (find) this job. What about you?

10 Choose the correct responses.

1. **A:** Are you from Toronto?
   B: _No, I'm originally from Morocco._
      - No, I'm originally from Morocco.
      - Neither am I.

2. **A:** Tell me a little about yourself.
   B: _____
      - Sure. Nice to meet you.
      - What do you want to know?

3. **A:** How old were you when you moved here?
   B: _____
      - About 16.
      - About 16 years ago.

4. **A:** Did you learn English here?
   B: _____
      - Yes, I was 10 years old.
      - No, I studied it in Morocco.

5. **A:** By the way, I'm Lucy.
   B: _____
      - What's your name?
      - Glad to meet you.

1 Choose the correct compound noun for each picture.

- ☐ bicycle lane
- ☐ subway station
- ☐ taxi stand
- ☐ bus stop
- ☑ streetlights
- ☐ traffic jam

1. <u>streetlights</u>

2. _____

3. _____

4. _____

5. _____

6. _____

2 Problems, problems

A Choose a solution for each problem.

Problems

1. no more parking spaces: _build a public parking garage_

2. dark streets: _____

3. no places to take children: _____

4. crime: _____

5. car accidents: _____

6. traffic jams: _____

Solutions

☐ install modern streetlights
☐ build a subway system
☐ install more traffic lights
☐ hire more police officers
☐ build more parks
☑ build a public parking garage

B Look at these solutions. Write sentences explaining the problems.
Use *too much, too many,* or *not enough* and the problems in part A.

1. _There aren't enough parking spaces._

   The city should build a public parking garage.

2. _____

   The city should install more traffic lights.

3. _____

   The city should build a subway system.

4. _____

   The city should hire more police officers.

5. _____

   The city should build more parks.

6. _____

   The city should install modern streetlights.

C Find another way to say the problems in part B. Begin each sentence
with *There should be more/less/fewer . . .*

1. _There should be more parking spaces._

2. _____

3. _____

4. _____

5. _____

6. _____

3 City blues

A Match the words in columns A and B. Write the compound nouns.

A	B	
☑ air	☐ district	**1.** _air pollution_
☐ business	☐ garages	**2.** _____
☐ green	☐ hour	**3.** _____
☐ parking	☐ spaces	**4.** _____
☐ bicycle	☐ lanes	**5.** _____
☐ public	☑ pollution	**6.** _____
☐ rush	☐ transportation	**7.** _____

B Complete this online post using the compound nouns in part A.

CITY FORUM   HOME | HEADLINES | LOCAL NEWS | INTERNATIONAL | BUSINESS | SPORTS | CONTACT US

Life in this city needs to be improved. For one thing, there are too many cars, and there is too much bad air, especially during _____rush hour_____. The _____ is terrible. This problem is particularly bad downtown in the _____.
Too many people drive their cars to work. Also, the city doesn't spend enough money on _____. There should be more buses and subway trains so people don't have to drive.

We also need fewer _____ downtown. It's so easy to park that too many people drive to work. Instead, the city should create more parks and _____ so people can relax and get some fresh air when they're downtown. There should also be more _____ so people can ride to work and get some exercise.

C Write two paragraphs about a problem in a city you know.
First describe the problem and then suggest solutions.

_____

_____

_____

_____

_____

_____

_____

_____

_____

4 Transportation in Hong Kong

A Read about transportation in Hong Kong. Write the correct types of transportation in the article.

GETTING AROUND HONG KONG

Hong Kong has an excellent transportation system. If you fly there, you will arrive at one of the most modern airports in the world. And during your visit, there are many ways to get around Hong Kong.

tram

subway

cable railway

ferry

1. _____

These have run in the streets of Hong Kong Island since 1904. They have two decks, and they carry more than 180,000 passengers a day. You can travel on six routes, totaling 30 kilometers (about 19 miles). You can also hire one for a private party with up to 25 guests – a great way to enjoy Hong Kong!

2. _____

Take one of these to cross from Hong Kong Island to Kowloon or to visit one of the other islands. You can also use them to travel to Macau and Guangdong. They are very safe and comfortable, and they are one of the cheapest boat rides in the world.

3. _____

Hong Kong's underground railway is called the MTR – the Mass Transit Railway. It is the fastest way to get around. You can take the MTR from the airport to all the major centers in Hong Kong. The MTR carries over four million passengers a day!

4. _____

This is found on Hong Kong Island. It pulls you up Victoria Peak, which is 552 meters (about 1,800 feet) above sea level, the highest mountain on the island. The system is nearly 130 years old. In that time, there has never been an accident. Two cars carry up to 120 passengers each.

B Complete the chart about each type of transportation. Where you cannot find the information, write *NG* (not given).

	cable railway	ferry	subway	tram
1. How old is it?	_____	_____	_____	_____
2. How many people use it?	_____	_____	_____	_____
3. How safe is it?	_____	_____	_____	_____
4. Where can you go?	_____	_____	_____	_____

5 Complete these conversations. Use the words in the box.

☐ ATM   ☑ duty-free shop   ☐ sign   ☐ hotel   ☐ schedule

1. A: Could you tell me where I can buy some perfume?

   B: You should try the _duty-free shop_ .

2. A: Can you tell me where I can find a good place to stay?

   B: Yeah, there is a nice _____
    on the next street.

3. A: Do you know where I can change money?

   B: There's a money exchange on the second floor.
    There's also an _____ over there.

4. A: Do you know what time the last train leaves for
    the city?

   B: No, but I can check the _____ .

5. A: Could you tell me where the taxi stand is?

   B: Sure. Just follow that _____ .

6 Complete the questions in this conversation at a hotel.

Guest: Could you _tell me where the gym is_ _____ ?

Clerk: Sure, the gym is on the nineteenth floor.

Guest: OK. And can you _____ ?

Clerk: Yes, the coffee shop is next to the gift shop.

Guest: The gift shop? Hmm. I need to buy something for my wife.
   Do you _____ ?

Clerk: It closes at 6:00 P.M. I'm sorry, but you'll have to wait until tomorrow.
   It's already 6:15.

Guest: OK. Oh, I'm expecting a package.
   Could you _____ ?

Clerk: Don't worry. I'll call you when it arrives.

Guest: Thanks. Just one more thing.
   Do you _____ ?

Clerk: The airport bus leaves every half hour. Anything else?

Guest: No, I don't think so. Thanks.

7 Rewrite these sentences. Find another way to say each sentence using the words given.

1. There are too many cars in this city. (fewer)

   There should be fewer cars in this city.

2. We need fewer buses and cars downtown. (traffic)

3. Where's the subway station? (Could you)

4. There isn't enough public parking. (parking garages)

5. How often does the bus come? (Do you)

6. What time does the last train leave? (Can you)

8 Answer these questions about your city or another city you know.

The streets are closed to traffic in a traffic-free zone.

1. Are there any traffic-free zones? If so, where are they located?

2. How do most people travel to and from work?

3. What's the rush hour like?

4. What's the city's biggest problem?

5. What has the city done about it?

6. Is there anything else the city could do?

3 Making changes

1 Opposites

A Write the opposites. Use the words in the box.

☐ dark	☐ old
☐ expensive	☐ safe
☑ inconvenient	☐ small
☐ noisy	☐ spacious

1. convenient / _inconvenient_
2. cramped / _____
3. dangerous / _____
4. big / _____

5. bright / _____
6. modern / _____
7. quiet / _____
8. cheap / _____

B Rewrite these sentences. Find another way to say each sentence using *not . . . enough* or *too* and the words in part A.

1. The house is too expensive.
   The house isn't cheap enough.

2. The rooms aren't bright enough.
   _____

3. The living room isn't spacious enough for the family.
   _____
   _____

4. The bathroom is too old.
   _____

5. The yard isn't big enough for our pets.
   _____

6. The street is too noisy for us.
   _____

7. The neighborhood is too dangerous.
   _____

8. The location isn't convenient enough.
   _____

2 Add the word *enough* to these sentences.

1. The apartment isn't comfortable ∧ *enough*.

2. There aren't bedrooms.

3. It's not modern.

4. There aren't parking spaces.

5. The neighborhood doesn't have streetlights.

6. There aren't closets.

7. It's not private.

8. The living room isn't spacious.

3 Complete this conversation. Use the words given and the comparisons in the box. (Some of the comparisons in the box can be used more than once.)

almost as . . . as   just as many . . . as
as many . . . as   not as . . . as

Realtor: How did you like the house on Twelfth Street?

Client: Well, it's ____*not as convenient as*____ the apartment on Main Street. (convenient)

Realtor: That's true, the house is less convenient.

Client: But the apartment doesn't have

_____ the house. (rooms)

Realtor: Yes, the house is more spacious.

Client: But I think there are _____
in the apartment. (closets)

Realtor: You're right. The closet space is the same.

Client: The wallpaper in the apartment is

_____ the wallpaper in

the house. (dingy)

Realtor: I know, but you could change the wallpaper in
the house.

Client: Hmm, the rent on the apartment is

_____ the rent on the

house, but the house is much bigger. (expensive)
Oh, I can't decide. Can you show me
something else?

4 Home, sweet home

A Complete this questionnaire about where you live, and find your score below.

How does your home measure up?

The outside
Yes No

1. Are you close enough to shopping?
2. Is there enough public transportation nearby?
3. Are the sidewalks clean?
4. Are there good restaurants in the neighborhood?
5. Is there a park nearby?
6. Is the neighborhood quiet?
7. Is the neighborhood safe?
8. Is there enough parking nearby?
9. Does the outside of your home look good?

The inside

10. Are there enough bedrooms?
11. Is there enough closet space?
12. Is the bathroom modern?
13. Is there a washing machine?
14. Is there enough space in the kitchen?
15. Do the stove and refrigerator work well?
16. Is the living room comfortable enough?
17. Is the dining area big enough?
18. Are the walls newly painted?
19. Are the rooms bright enough?
20. Is the building warm enough in cold weather?

To score:
How many "Yes" answers do you have?

16–20
It sounds like a dream home!

11–15
Great! All you need now is a swimming pool!

6–10
Well, at least guests won't want to stay long!

0–5
It's time to look for a better place to live!

B Write two short paragraphs about where you live. In the first paragraph describe your neighborhood, and in the second paragraph describe your home. Use the information in part A or your own information.

_____
_____
_____
_____
_____
_____
_____
_____

5 Wishes

A Which words or phrases often go with which verbs? Complete the chart.

☐ guitar	☐ happier	☐ my own room	☐ soccer
☐ more free time	☑ healthy	☐ somewhere else	☐ to a new place

be	play	have	move
___healthy___	_____	_____	_____
_____	_____	_____	_____

B Describe what these people would like to change. Use *I wish* and words or phrases in part A.

1. I wish I were healthy.

2. _____

3. _____

4. _____

5. _____

6. _____

6 Choose the correct responses.

1. A: I wish I had a bigger apartment.

   B: _Why?_

   • Why?

   • I don't like my neighbors, either.

2. A: I wish I could retire.

   B: _____

   • I don't like it anymore.

   • I know what you mean.

3. A: Where do you want to move?

   B: _____

   • Somewhere else.

   • Something else.

4. A: I wish I could find a bigger house.

   B: _____

   • Is it too large?

   • It's very nice, though.

7 Rewrite these sentences. Find another way to say each sentence using the words given.

1. There should be more bedrooms in my apartment. (enough)

   There aren't enough bedrooms in my apartment.

2. This neighborhood is safe enough. (dangerous)

   _____

3. My apartment doesn't have enough privacy. (private)

   _____

4. Our house has the same number of bedrooms as yours. (just as many)

   _____

5. I don't have enough closet space. (wish)

   _____

6. We wish we could move to a new place. (somewhere else)

   _____

7. That apartment is too small. (big)

   _____

8. I wish housework were easy. (not difficult)

   _____

8 Best wishes

A Scan the article about making wishes. Which three countries does it refer to?

MAKING WISHES

All over the world, people have always wished for things such as peace, love, good health, and money. Over hundreds of years, people in different countries have found different ways to make wishes. Here are some interesting examples.

The Trevi Fountain in Rome, Italy, is a place where many people go to make a wish. The water from the fountain flows into a large pool of water below. To make a wish, visitors stand facing away from the fountain. Then, they use their right hand to throw a coin into the pool over their left shoulder. They believe this will bring them luck and bring them back to Rome one day. The coins in the fountain, several thousand euros each day, are given to poor people.

A very different way of making wishes happens in Anhui province in eastern China. Huangshan (which means "Yellow Mountain") is famous for its beautiful sunrises and sunsets. That's why people think it is a very romantic place. Couples go there to make a wish that they will stay together forever. Each couple buys a "love lock," or padlock, with a key. Next, they lock their padlock to a chain at the top of the mountain. Then they throw the key down the mountain so that their lock can never be opened.

In Turkey and some neighboring countries, May 5th is a special day for making wishes. People believe that each year on that day two wise men return to Earth. They come to help people and give them good health. In the evening, there are street food markets selling different kinds of seasonal food and musicians playing traditional music. People write their wishes on pieces of paper and then attach the paper to a tree. Nowadays, however, some people go online and send their wishes to special websites.

B Read the article. Check (✓) the statements that are true for each place.

	Rome	Huangshan	Turkey
1. People make wishes only once a year.	☐	☐	☐
2. You need a lock and key.	☐	☐	☐
3. You put your wish on a tree.	☐	☐	☐
4. You need a coin to make your wish.	☐	☐	☐
5. Wish-making is only for couples.	☐	☐	☐
6. The money from the wishes goes to poor people.	☐	☐	☐
7. Some people make their wishes on the Internet.	☐	☐	☐

4 Have you ever tried it?

1 Complete the conversation with the correct tense.

Margo: I went to Sunrise Beach last week.

Have you ever been
(Did you ever go / Have you ever been)

to Sunrise Beach, Chris?

Chris: Yes, _____. It's beautiful.
(I did / I have)

_____
(Did you go / Have you gone)

to the restaurant on the beach?

Margo: Yeah, I _____.
(did / have)

I _____ on Saturday.
(went / have gone)

_____ the sea snails.
(I had / I've had)

Chris: Wow! _____ sea snails!
(I never ate / I've never eaten)

Margo: Oh, they were delicious. On Sunday

I _____
(got / have gotten)

to the beach early to see the sun come up.

_____ a sunrise on a beach, Chris?
(Did you ever see / Have you ever seen)

Chris: No, _____.
(I didn't / I haven't)

Margo: Then I _____ swimming around 6:00,
(went / have gone)

but there were some strange dark shadows in the water.

_____ of sharks at Sunrise Beach?
(Did you ever hear / Have you ever heard)

Chris: Yes, _____. I _____ a news report about sharks last summer.
(I did / I have)   (heard / have heard)

Margo: Wow! Maybe I _____ a lucky escape on Sunday morning!
(had / have had)

Why don't you come with me next time?

Chris: Are you kidding?

2 Have you ever . . . ?

A Look at this list and check (✓) five things you have done. Add other activities if necessary.

- ☐ ride a motorcycle
- ☐ go horseback riding
- ☐ cook for over 10 people
- ☐ eat raw fish
- ☐ go to a classical music concert
- ✓ have green tea ice cream
- ☐ read a novel in English
- ☐ take a cruise
- ☐ travel abroad
- ☐ try Indian food
- ☐ _____
- ☐ _____
- ☐ _____
- ☐ _____

B Write questions about the things you checked in part A. Use *Have you ever . . . ?*

1. _Have you ever had green tea ice cream?_ _____

2. _____

3. _____

4. _____

5. _____

C Answer the questions you wrote in part B. Then use the past tense to give more information.

1. _Yes, I have. I had some in a Japanese restaurant. It was delicious!_ _____

2. _____

3. _____

4. _____

5. _____

3 Do I have an allergy?

A Scan the article. What can cause allergies?

ALLERGIES

ANDREW was sneezing all of the time. He took an aspirin every morning for a week before he decided to see a doctor. She told him that he had hay fever, an allergy to the pollen from the juniper trees that grew in the area where Andrew lived. The doctor suggested an anti-allergy medicine that he had to take three times a day. But Andrew didn't get completely well until he also bought an air filter to clean the air in his apartment.

MARIANA loved her cat Lucy very much, but her eyes were always red and irritated. She discovered she had an allergy to her cat! She tried to pet Lucy less, but that didn't work. Her friends advised her to give Lucy away, but Mariana couldn't do that. Instead she changed where Lucy could go. Lucy was no longer allowed in Mariana's bedroom. Mariana made a little bed for Lucy in the garage. Mariana played with her cat outside because fresh air is best for cat allergies.

It was a very sad day when **ERIC'S** mother told him he shouldn't eat his favorite food anymore. He had a food allergy, she said, and peanut butter was the problem. Peanuts made his skin very red with a painful itch. Eric tried to eat less peanut butter, but he still itched. Now Eric eats almond butter, cashew butter, and tahini, which is also called sesame butter. A lot of his friends also eat these foods since Eric's school no longer serves peanut butter because of peanut allergies.

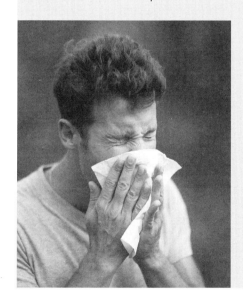

B Read the article. What problem did each person have? Complete the first column of the chart.

	Problem	What didn't work	What worked
Andrew	_____	_____	_____
Mariana	_____	_____	_____
Eric	_____	_____	_____

C Read the article again. What didn't work? What worked? Complete the rest of the chart.

4 Eggs, anyone?

A Here's a recipe for a mushroom omelet. Look at the pictures and number the sentences from 1 to 5.

_____ After that, pour the eggs into a frying pan. Add the mushrooms and cook.

_____ Then beat the eggs in a bowl.

_1_ First, slice the mushrooms.

_____ Next, add salt and pepper to the egg mixture.

_____ Finally, fold the omelet in half. Your omelet is ready. Enjoy!

B Describe your favorite way to cook eggs. Use sequence adverbs.

HOW TO COOK EGGS:

5 Complete the conversation. Use the past tense or the present perfect of the verbs given.

Alexa: I _____went_____ (go) to a Thai restaurant last night.

Pedro: Really? I _____ (never eat) Thai food.

Alexa: Oh, you should try it. It's delicious!

Pedro: What _____ you _____ (order)?

Alexa: First, I _____ (have) soup with green curry and rice. Then I _____ (try) pad thai. It's noodles, shrimp, and vegetables in a spicy sauce.

Pedro: I _____ (not taste) pad thai before. _____ (be) it very hot?

Alexa: No. It _____ (be) just spicy enough. And after that, I _____ (eat) bananas in coconut milk for dessert.

Pedro: Mmm! That sounds good.

Alexa: It was.

6 Choose the correct word.

1. We had delicious guacamole dip and chips on Saturday night while we watched TV. It was a great _____snack_____ (dinner / snack / meal).

2. I had a huge lunch, so I _____ (ordered / skipped / tried) dinner.

3. What _____ (appetizers / ingredients / skewers) do you need to cook crispy fried noodles?

4. First, fry the beef in oil and curry powder, and then _____ (pour / mix / toast) the coconut milk over the beef.

5. We need to leave the restaurant now. Could we have the _____ (check / recipe / menu), please?

7 Choose the correct responses.

☐ Yuck! That sounds awful.   ☐ That sounds wrong.   ☐ Mmm! That sounds good.

1. A: Have you ever tried barbecued chicken? You marinate the meat in
   barbecue sauce for about an hour and then cook it on the grill.

   B: _____

2. A: Here's a recipe called Baked Eggplant Delight. I usually bake eggplant
   for an hour, but this says you bake it for only five minutes!

   B: _____

3. A: Look at this dish – frogs' legs with bananas! I've never seen that before.

   B: _____

8 Use the simple past or present perfect of these verbs to complete the sentences.

☑ ride   ☐ take   ☐ bring   ☐ do

1. Have you ever ____ridden____ a horse? It's great!
2. I _____ all the ingredients with me.
3. _____ you eat a huge dinner last night?
4. We _____ my mother to the new Chilean restaurant.

☐ give   ☐ decide   ☐ eat   ☐ be

5. I haven't _____ a birthday gift to my father yet.
6. We have never _____ to a Chinese restaurant.
7. I have never _____ snails. What are they like?
8. Have you _____ what kind of pizza you would like?

☐ make   ☐ break   ☐ buy   ☐ skip

9. I _____ this chicken sandwich for $5.
10. Oh, I'm sorry. I just _____ a glass. What a mess!
11. Victor _____ gogi gui for dinner.
12. I wasn't hungry this morning, so I _____ breakfast.

☐ fall   ☐ forget   ☐ drive   ☐ try

13. Oh, no! I _____ to buy rice.
14. Have you ever _____ a sports car?
15. I _____ Greek food for the first time last night.
16. Have you ever _____ asleep at the movies? It's really embarrassing.

5 Hit the road!

Vacation plans

A Which words or phrases often go with which verbs? Complete the chart.
Use each word or phrase only once.

- [ ] a camper
- [ ] camping
- [ ] something exciting
- [✓] long walks
- [ ] a lot of hiking
- [ ] some fishing
- [ ] a condominium
- [ ] on vacation
- [ ] sailing lessons
- [ ] a car
- [ ] swimming
- [ ] a vacation

take	do	go	rent
long walks			

B Write four things you plan to do on your next vacation. Use *be going to* and
the information in part A or your own information.

Vacation plans

1. _____
2. _____
3. _____
4. _____

C Write four sentences about your possible vacation plans. Use *will* with *maybe*,
probably, *I guess*, or *I think*. Use the information in part A or your own information.

Possible plans

1. _____
2. _____
3. _____
4. _____

2 Complete the conversation. Use *be going to* or *will* and the information on the notepads.

Scott: So, Elena, do you have any vacation plans?

Elena: Well, ___I'm going to paint my apartment___ because the walls are a really ugly color. What about you?

Scott: _____ and take a long drive.

Elena: Where are you going to go?

Scott: I'm not sure. _____.
I haven't seen her in a long time.

Elena: That sounds nice. I like to visit my family, too.

Scott: Yes, and _____
for a few days. I haven't been hiking in months.
How about you? Are you going to do anything else on your vacation?

Elena: _____. I have a lot of work to do before school starts.

Scott: That doesn't sound like much fun.

Elena: Oh, I am planning to have some fun, too.
_____. I love to go surfing!

Elena
paint my apartment – yes
catch up on my studying – probably
relax on the beach – yes

Scott
rent a car – yes
visit my sister Jeanne – probably
go to the mountains – maybe

3 Travel plans

A Look at these answers. Write questions using *be going to*.

1. A: _Where are you going to go?_
   B: I'm going to go someplace nice and quiet.

2. A: _____
   B: I'm going to drive.

3. A: _____
   B: I'm going to stay in a condominium. My friend has one near the beach.

4. A: _____
   B: No, I'm going to travel by myself.

B Use the cues to write other answers to the questions in part A. Use *be going to* or *will*.

1. _I'm not going to go to a busy place._ (not go / busy place)

2. _____ (maybe / take the train)

3. _____ (not stay / hotel)

4. _____ (I think / ask a friend)

Travel ads

A Scan the travel ad. Where can tourists see beautiful nature scenes?

● ● ● ‹ ›

http://www.holidayofalifetime.com

THE PERFECT SOUTH AMERICAN VACATION ● **SEE TWO EXCITING CITIES AND ONE OF SOUTH AMERICA'S NATURAL WONDERS** ● **11 DAYS FOR $1,199 + AIRFARE!**

BUENOS AIRES

In this unique city of art, culture, and history, there are over 150 parks, 42 theaters, and museums and shops everywhere. You must visit Avenida 9 de Julio, the widest avenue in the world. The food is excellent, and you simply have to try the steaks! The home of the tango also offers great nightlife – all night long!

RIO DE JANEIRO

There's a lot to do in this exciting city! There's opera and ballet as well as museums, churches, parks, and great beaches. Just outside of the city, there are the Sugarloaf and Corcovado Mountains. Dining starts late in Rio, around 9:00 P.M., and dancing in the clubs begins around 11:00 P.M.

IGUAÇU FALLS

Bigger than Niagara Falls, this is truly an unforgettable wonder. For a real adventure, you ought to take a boat ride. And you must explore the national parks near the falls.

Book with FLIGHT and SAVE!
Reserve online, or call **1-800-555-TRIP** for more information.

B Read the ad. Check (✓) True or False. For the statements that are false, write the correct information.

	True	False
1. People have dinner late in Rio de Janeiro.	☐	☐
2. Buenos Aires has the longest avenue in the world.	☐	☐
3. Niagara Falls is bigger than Iguaçu Falls.	☐	☐
4. Both Rio de Janeiro and Buenos Aires have exciting nightlife.	☐	☐
5. Buenos Aires and Iguaçu Falls have great beaches.	☐	☐

Hit the road! **27**

5 Circle the correct word or words to give advice to travelers.

1. You ought (check /(to check)) the weather.
2. You should never (leave / to leave) cash in your hotel room.
3. You need (take / to take) your credit card with you.
4. You have (pay / to pay) an airport tax.
5. You should (let / to let) your family know where they can contact you.
6. You'd better not (go / to go) out alone late at night.
7. You must (get / to get) a vaccination if you go to some countries.

6 Take it or leave it?

A Check (✓) the most important item to have in each situation.

1. A vacation to a foreign country
   - ☐ a carry-on bag
   - ☑ a passport
   - ☐ a driver's license

2. A mountain-climbing vacation
   - ☐ a suitcase
   - ☐ a visa
   - ☐ hiking boots

3. A sailing trip
   - ☐ a hotel reservation
   - ☐ a first-aid kit
   - ☐ an ATM card

4. A visit to a beach
   - ☐ a credit card
   - ☐ a swimsuit
   - ☐ a plane ticket

B Give advice to these people. Use the words or phrases in the box and the items in part A. Use each word or phrase only once.

☐ ought to   ☐ need to   ☐ should   ☑ had better ('d better)

1. Martina is going on a vacation to a foreign country.
   She'd better take a passport.

2. Robin and Evan are going on a mountain-climbing vacation.
   _____

3. Kevin and Susie are planning a sailing trip.
   _____

4. Eddie is going to visit a beach.
   _____

7 You don't need to take that!

Your friends are planning to drive across North America and camp along the way. What advice can you give them? Write sentences using the expressions in the box and some of the cues below.

You don't have to . . .	You ought to . . .
You have to . . .	You should . . .
You must . . .	You shouldn't . . .
You need to . . .	You'd better . . .

bring cooking equipment

buy good quality camping equipment

buy maps and travel guides

forget a first-aid kit

forget your passport or identification

get a GPS device for your car

pack a lot of luggage

remember to bring insect spray

remember to bring a jacket

take a credit card

take a lot of cash

take your driver's license

1. *You have to bring cooking equipment.*
2. _____
3. _____
4. _____
5. _____
6. _____
7. _____
8. _____
9. _____
10. _____

8 Rewrite these sentences. Find another way to say each sentence using the words given.

1. I'm not going to go on vacation on my own. (alone)

   _____

2. I don't want to travel with anyone. (by myself)

   _____

3. You ought to travel with a friend. (should)

   _____

4. It's necessary to get a vaccination. (must)

   _____

9 I'm going on vacation!

A Read these notes, and then write a description of your vacation.
Use *be going to* for the plans you've decided on. Use *will* with *maybe*,
probably, *I guess*, or *I think* for the plans you're not sure about.

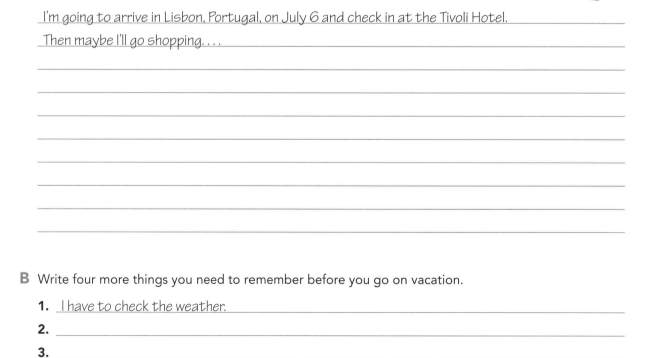

- arrive in Lisbon, Portugal, on July 6
- check in at the Tivoli Hotel
- go shopping (not sure)
- spend three days in Lisbon sightseeing
- take a tour bus across the border to Seville in Spain
- visit the cathedral (not sure)
- see some flamenco dancing in the evening
- rent a car and drive to Málaga on the Costa del Sol
- visit the old city center (not sure)
- spend time on the beach (not sure)
- fly to Madrid on July 19
- visit some museums (not sure)
- take a tour of the city and see the sights
- go home on July 22

I'm going to arrive in Lisbon, Portugal, on July 6 and check in at the Tivoli Hotel.
Then maybe I'll go shopping. . . .

B Write four more things you need to remember before you go on vacation.

1. I have to check the weather.
2.
3.
4.
5.

6 Sure! I'll do it.

1 Write responses to these requests. Use *it* or *them*.

1. Please take out the trash.

   OK, I'll take it out.

2. Please put the dishes away.

   _____

3. Hang up the towels.

   _____

4. Turn off the lights, please.

   _____

5. Turn on the radio.

   _____

2 Two-part verbs

A Use the words in the box to make two-part verbs. (You may use words more than once.)

away	down	off	on	out	up

1. clean _____up_____
2. hang _____
3. let _____
4. pick _____
5. put _____

6. take _____
7. take _____
8. throw _____
9. turn _____
10. turn _____

B Make requests with the two-part verbs in part A. Then give a reason for making the request.

1. Please clean up your room. It's a mess.
2. _____
3. _____
4. _____
5. _____
6. _____

3 Choose the correct word.

1. Hang up your _____coat_____. (books / coat / trash)

2. Take out the _____. (groceries / trash / yard)

3. Turn down the _____. (garbage / TV / toys)

4. Pick up your _____. (lights / things / yard)

5. Put away your _____. (clothes / microwave / dog)

6. Turn on the _____. (magazines / mess / radio)

4 What's your excuse?

A Complete these requests. Use the sentences in the box.

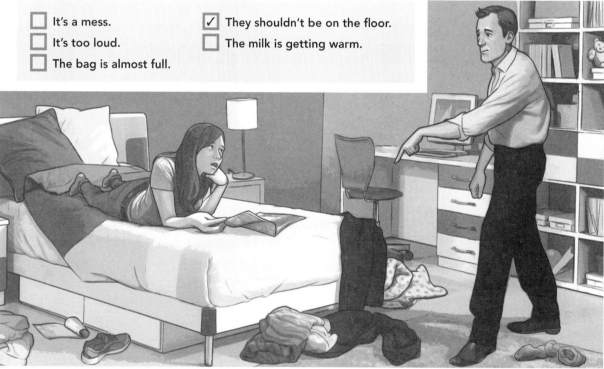

☐ It's a mess.   ☑ They shouldn't be on the floor.
☐ It's too loud.   ☐ The milk is getting warm.
☐ The bag is almost full.

1. Pick up your clothes, please. _They shouldn't be on the floor._

2. Please put the groceries away. _____

3. Take the garbage out. _____

4. Clean up the kitchen, please. _____

5. Turn down the music. _____

B Write an excuse for each request in part A.

1. _Sorry, but there isn't enough room in my closet._

2. _____

3. _____

4. _____

5. _____

5 Two ways to get chores done

A Scan this article. What is different about the two computer apps for children's chores?

ChoreMonster is an app that allows parents to set up a chart of chores on a computer or cell phone for their children. When the kids complete their chores, they win cute little monsters that can be added up for a reward that their parents have agreed upon. For chores like cleaning their room, vacuuming the house, or washing the car, kids can earn a toy or something fun to do.

But wait! Will the cute little monsters that satisfy children between the ages of four and twelve satisfy a teenager? Let's take a look at another app to see what can happen when children become teenagers.

VexBox is not an app based on rewards. Instead, it is designed to frustrate, or vex, teenagers who don't do their chores. VexBox slows down computer connections until the teen completes a chore. It can take teenagers ten minutes to download their favorite song! The idea is that teens will do anything, even their chores, so they can get back to using the Internet at full speed.

Most teens do not like VexBox. That's the idea, of course. If they do their chores, then their parents won't use it!

B Read the article. Then answer these questions in your own words.

1. Do you think computer apps for chores are a good idea? Why or why not?

_____

_____

2. Would you use ChoreMonster for a young child? Why or why not?

_____

_____

3. Smartphones are not affected by VexBox. Would that be a problem for parents with teenagers where you live? Why?

_____

_____

6 Rewrite these sentences. Find another way to say each sentence using the words given.

1. Turn off your cell phone, please. (Can)

   Can you turn off your cell phone, please?

2. Take this form to the office. (Would you mind)

   _____

3. Please turn the TV down. (Could)

   _____

4. Don't leave wet towels on the floor. (Would you mind)

   _____

5. Text me today's homework assignment. (Would)

   _____

6. Pass me that book, please. (Can)

   _____

7 Choose the correct responses.

1. **A:** Could you lend me some money?

   B: _Sure._

   • Sure.

   • Oh, sorry.

   • No, thanks.

2. **A:** Would you mind helping me?

   B: _____

   • Sorry, I can't right now.

   • No, thanks.

   • I forgot.

3. **A:** Excuse me, but you're sitting in my seat.

   B: _____

   • I'll close it.

   • Not right now.

   • Oh, I'm sorry. I didn't realize that.

4. **A:** Would you like to come in?

   B: _____

   • That's no excuse.

   • Sorry, I forgot.

   • All right. Thanks.

5. **A:** Would you mind not leaving your clothes on the floor?

   B: _____

   • OK, thanks.

   • Oh, all right. I'll put them away.

   • Excuse me. I'll pay for them.

6. **A:** Can you hand me the remote control?

   B: _____

   • No problem.

   • You could, too.

   • I'll make sure.

8 For each complaint, apologize and either give an excuse, admit a mistake, make an offer, or make a promise.

1. **Roommate 1:** Could you turn the TV down? I'm trying to study, and the noise is bothering me.

   Roommate 2: *Sorry. I didn't realize you were studying.*

2. **Benjamin:** You're late! I've been here for half an hour!

   Jen: _____

3. **Customer:** I brought this laptop in last week, but it's still not working right.

   Salesperson: _____

4. **Father:** You didn't take out the garbage this morning.

   Son: _____

5. **Customer:** This steak is very tough. I can't eat it.

   Waiter: _____

6. **Neighbor 1:** Could you do something about your dog? It barks all night and it keeps me awake.

   Neighbor 2: _____

7. **Resident:** Would you mind moving your car? You're parked in my parking space.

   Visitor: _____

8. **Teacher:** Please put away your papers. You left them on your desk yesterday.

   Student: _____

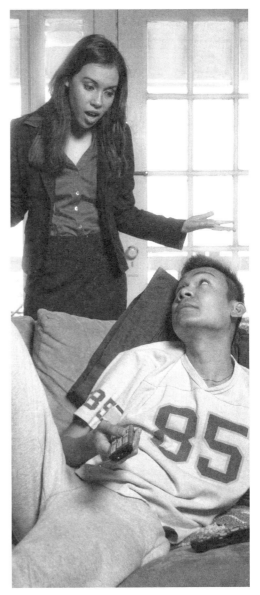

9 Choose the correct words.

1. Throw that old food away. Put it in the _____.
   (trash can / living room / refrigerator)

2. Would you mind picking up some _____? We need coffee, milk, and rice.
   (dry cleaning / groceries / towels)

3. Turn the _____ off. Electricity costs money!
   (lights / oven / stereo)

4. My neighbor made a _____. He said, "I'll be sure to stop my dog from barking."
   (mistake / request / promise)

10 Make requests

A Match the words in columns A and B. Then write the phrases.

A	B
☑ pick up	☐ your bedroom
☐ not criticize	☑ some milk
☐ mail	☐ the groceries
☐ not talk	☐ your sunglasses
☐ put away	☐ these bills
☐ take off	☐ the TV
☐ turn down	☐ so loudly
☐ clean up	☐ my friends

1. _pick up some milk_
2. _____
3. _____
4. _____
5. _____
6. _____
7. _____
8. _____

B Write requests using the phrases in part A.

1. _Would you mind picking up some milk?_
2. _____
3. _____
4. _____
5. _____
6. _____
7. _____
8. _____

11 Write six complaints you have about a friend or a relative. Then write a wish for each complaint.

1. _My roommate is always using my hair dryer._
    I wish she had her own hair dryer.
2. _____
    _____
3. _____
    _____
4. _____
    _____
5. _____
    _____
6. _____
    _____

7 What do you use this for?

1

What are these items used for? Write a sentence about each item using *used for* and the information in the box.

- [ ] do boring jobs
- [ ] store and send data
- [ ] take and delete photos easily
- [✓] write reports
- [ ] determine your exact location

computer   robot   digital camera   flash drive   GPS device

1. _A computer is used for writing reports._

2. _____

3. _____

4. _____

5. _____

2

Check (✓) the technology and its use. Then write sentences using *be used to.*

1. [✓] text messages   [✓] cell phone   [ ] photocopies

A cell phone is used to send text messages.

2. [ ] flash drive   [ ] take photos   [ ] back up files

_____

3. [ ] weather   [ ] GPS device   [ ] places

_____

4. [ ] videos   [ ] messages   [ ] video camera

_____

5. [ ] the Internet   [ ] robots   [ ] information

_____

3 Choose the correct word to complete each sentence. Use the correct form of the word.

1. Robots are used to ____perform____ (find / perform / study) many dangerous jobs.

2. Computers are used to _____ (connect / download / sing) music.

3. The Internet is used for _____ (check / watch / write) streaming TV.

4. Home computers are used to _____ (play / pay / have) bills.

5. External hard drives are used for _____ (back up / email / buy) data.

6. Airport scanners are used to _____ (hide / allow / find) dangerous items.

4 Complete the sentences with *used to*, *is used to*, or *are used to*.

1. My sister _____used to_____ visit me on weekends when I was in college.

2. People _____ write letters, but now they usually send emails instead.

3. A cell phone _____ make calls and send texts.

4. I _____ have a desktop computer, but now I just use a laptop.

5. We download all of our movies. We _____ buy DVDs, but we don't buy them anymore.

6. Wi-Fi networks _____ access the Internet wirelessly.

5 Then and now

A Scan these ads from a sales catalog from 1917 and from a Web store a century later. What is different?

1917 CATALOG

DETROIT ELECTRIC AUTOMOBILE

So quiet because it does not need a gasoline engine. The large, high windows make you feel like you're sitting in your living room! Travels 80 miles without being recharged. $2,700.

VICTROLA PHONOGRAPH

The first thing you'll ask is, "Where's the speaker?" The Victrola has the speaker inside the cabinet! The beautiful wood of the cabinet makes the sound sweeter! $250.00.

AMERICAN EAGLE TELEPHONE

Allows you to talk easily to family and friends all over the country. Available with a wooden case and weighs less than 5 pounds. $25.00.

2017 WEB STORE

Aethera Electric Car

Has autopilot and automatic steering to allow you to drive safely. Travels 300 miles without recharging the battery. $43,000.

Big Sky Sound System

Allows streaming and plays compact discs so you can listen to all the music you love. Also included is a record player for your grandparents' records and the new ones you just bought! $299.00.

FutureNow Smartphone

Stay connected to everyone you know by telephone and on the Internet. This beautifully slender phone puts the whole world in your pocket. And it takes incredible photos! $799.00.

B Read the ads. Then answer these questions in your own words.

1. Would you buy a Detroit electric car today for use in your town or city? Why or why not?

2. Have you listened to music over the Internet, on CDs, and on records? Which do you think sounds the best? Why?

3. Although the American Eagle telephone is a hundred years old, is there anything about it that you like as much as today's smartphone?

6 Useful types of websites

A Match the types of websites with how people use them.

Types of websites	How people use websites
_d_ question and answer sites	**a.** find out what's happening in the world
_____ blogs	**b.** share information and photos with friends
_____ gaming sites	**c.** buy clothes, electronics, and other items
_____ media sharing sites	**d.** ask and answer questions online
_____ news sites	**e.** find information on the Internet
_____ search engines	**f.** play online games
_____ social media sites	**g.** post online diaries
_____ shopping sites	**h.** upload videos and music

B Do you use any of the types of websites in part A? What do you use them for? Write sentences.

1. _I use question and answer sites to ask and answer questions online._   OR
    I use question and answer sites for asking and answering questions online.

2. _____

3. _____

4. _____

7 Put these instructions in order. Number them from 1 to 5.

GETTING STARTED WITH SOCIAL NETWORKING

_____ Next, check what the site has to offer you. Don't worry if you can't understand all its functions.

_____ First of all, join a social networking site. Choose a site where you already know people.

_____ After that, use the site's search features to find friends. Be sure to browse through groups who share your interests.

_____ Finally, invite people to be your friend. Try not to be shy! A lot of people may be waiting to hear from you.

_____ Then customize your profile page. For example, play with the colors to make the page reflect your personality. Now you're ready to start exploring!

8 Write a sentence about each picture using an expression in the box.

- ☐ Be sure to . . .
- ☐ Make sure to . . .
- ☐ Try not to . . .
- ☑ Don't forget to . . .
- ☐ Remember to . . .
- ☐ Try to . . .

1. *Don't forget to turn off your computer.*

2. _____

3. _____

4. _____

5. _____

6. _____

9 Write *a* or *an* in the correct places. (There are nine other places in this paragraph.)

My brother just bought ∧*a* smartphone. It's really great. It has lot of high-tech features. In fact, it's amazing handheld computer, not just cell phone. For example, it has Wi-Fi connectivity, so my brother can connect to the Internet in most places. He can send message to friend by email or through social networking site. He can also find out where he is because it has GPS app. That's perfect for my brother because he likes mountain climbing. He'll never get lost again! His smartphone also has excellent camera, so he can take photos of his climbing trips. And, of course, it's phone. So he can talk to his girlfriend anytime he wants!

Rewrite these sentences. Find another way to say each sentence using the words given.

1. I use my computer for paying bills. (online)

   I pay my bills online.

2. It breaks very easily. (fragile)

   _____

3. Take it out of the outlet. (unplug)

   _____

4. Remember to keep it dry. (spill)

   _____

5. Don't let the battery die. (recharge)

   _____

Look at the pictures and complete this conversation. Choose the correct responses.

A: What a day! First, my microwave didn't work.

B: What happened?

A: _It burned my lunch._

   • It didn't cook my lunch.

   • It burned my lunch.

   Then I tried to use my computer, but that didn't work either.

B: Why not?

A: _____

   • I couldn't get a Wi-Fi signal.

   • I couldn't turn it on.

   After that, I tried to use the vacuum cleaner.

B: Let me guess. It didn't pick up the dirt.

A: Worse! _____

   • It made a terrible noise.

   • It spread dirt around the room.

B: Did you take the vacuum cleaner to get it fixed?

A: Well, I tried, _____

   • but my car wouldn't start.

   • but I forgot.

B: Oh, no! Do you need a ride to work tomorrow?

8 Time to celebrate!

1 Complete this paragraph with the words in the box.

☐ get together   ☐ music   ☐ fireworks   ☐ decorations
☑ holidays   ☐ customs   ☐ picnic   ☐ celebrate

One of the most important national ___holidays___ in the United States is Independence Day. This is the day when Americans _____ winning their independence from Britain almost 250 years ago. There are many _____ for Independence Day. Most towns, big and small, mark this holiday with parades and _____. They put up a lot of _____, usually in red, white, and blue, the colors of the U.S. flag. Bands play patriotic _____. It's also a day when many Americans _____ with family and friends to celebrate with a barbecue or a _____.

2 Complete the sentences with the clauses in the box.

☐ when I feel sad and depressed   ☐ when people have to pay their taxes
☐ when school starts   ☐ when summer vacation begins

1. I hate April 15! In the United States, it's the day
   _____.
   I always owe the government money.

2. June is my favorite month. It's the month
   _____.
   I always go straight to the beach.

3. September is my least favorite month. It's the month _____.
   Good-bye, summer!

4. I've never liked winter. It's a season
   _____. The cold weather always affects my mood negatively.

3 Special days

A Use words from the box to complete the sentences.

☐	February	☐	tricks
☑	June	☐	wedding
☐	anniversary	☐	presents
☐	party	☐	fireworks

1. _June_____ is the time of year when there are a lot of weddings in the U.S.

2. We always have a _____ at our house on New Year's Eve.

3. Janice and Nick are getting married soon. They plan to have a small _____ with just a few family members.

4. Valentine's Day is on _____ 14th every year.

5. My friends and family gave me some very nice _____ on my birthday.

6. People like to play _____ on each other on April Fools' Day.

7. On the Fourth of July, many people shoot _____ into the sky at night.

8. Tomorrow is my parents' 25th wedding _____ .

B Use the cues in parentheses to create sentences with relative clauses of time.

1. (Thanksgiving / a day / people spend time with their families)
   Thanksgiving is a day when people spend time with their families.

2. (Spring / the season / flowers start to bloom)
   _____

3. (New Year's Eve / a night / people celebrate new beginnings)
   _____

4. (The weekend / a time / people relax)
   _____

5. (Father's Day / a day / children spend time with their fathers)
   _____

6. (Winter / the season / we go skiing)
   _____

A lot to celebrate!

A Read about these special days in the United States. Do you celebrate any of them in your country?

EVENT		DAY	HOW PEOPLE CELEBRATE IT
	Martin Luther King Jr. Day	3rd Monday in January	People honor the life and work of the civil rights leader Martin Luther King Jr.
	Valentine's Day	February 14th	People give chocolates, flowers, and gifts to the ones they love.
	April Fools' Day	April 1st	This is a day when people play tricks on friends. Websites sometimes post funny stories or advertise fake products.
	Mother's Day	2nd Sunday in May	People honor their mothers by giving cards and gifts. They may also have a family gathering.
	Father's Day	2nd Sunday in June	People honor their fathers by giving them cards and presents. They may also have a family gathering.
	Independence Day	July 4th	Americans celebrate their country's independence from Britain. There are parades and fireworks.
	Labor Day	1st Monday in September	People honor workers and celebrate the end of summer. Many people have barbecues with friends and family.
	Thanksgiving	4th Thursday in November	People celebrate the fall season by eating a big dinner, often with turkey, with family members and friends.

B Complete the chart. Check (✓) the correct answers.

	Americans give gifts on:	Americans don't give gifts on:
Martin Luther King Jr. Day	☐	☐
Valentine's Day	☐	☐
April Fools' Day	☐	☐
Mother's Day	☐	☐
Father's Day	☐	☐
Independence Day	☐	☐
Labor Day	☐	☐
Thanksgiving	☐	☐

5 What happens at these times in your country? Complete the sentences.

1. Before a man and woman get married, _they_
usually date each other.
_____

2. When someone has a birthday, _____
_____

3. After a couple moves into a new home, _____
_____

4. After a student graduates, _____
_____

5. When a woman gets engaged, _____
_____

6. When a couple has their first child, _____
_____

6 Complete the paragraph with the information in the box. Add a comma where necessary.

> **Grammar note: Adverbial clauses of time**
>
> **The adverbial clause can come <u>before</u> or <u>after</u> the main clause.**
> **If it comes <u>before</u> the main clause, add a comma.**
> *When a couple gets married, they often receive gifts.*
> **Do not add a comma <u>after</u> the main clause.**
> *A couple often receives gifts when they get married.*

- [ ] before the wedding reception ends
- [ ] many newlyweds have to live with relatives
- [ ] most couples like to be alone
- [ ] when they have enough money to pay for it

Newly married couples often leave on their honeymoon _____.
When they go on their honeymoon _____. After they come back
from their honeymoon _____. They can only live in their
own place _____.

7 Write three paragraphs about marriage customs in your country. In the first paragraph, write about what happens before the wedding. In the second paragraph, write about the wedding ceremony. In the final paragraph, write about what happens after the wedding.

_____

_____

_____

_____

_____

_____

_____

_____

_____

_____

Japan

Morocco

Scotland

India

8 Choose the correct word or phrase.

1. Wedding _____ (celebrations / flowers / birthdays) are often held in a restaurant or hotel.

2. Children's Day is a day when people in many countries _____ (meet / honor / find) their children.

3. Fall is the _____ (custom / tradition / season) when people in the U.S. celebrate Thanksgiving.

4. In Indonesia, on Nyepi Day, Balinese people _____ (last / stop / observe) a day of silence to begin the new year.

9 **Rewrite these sentences. Find another way to say each sentence using the words given.**

1. Everyone in the family comes to my parents' home on Thanksgiving. (get together)

   Everyone in the family gets together at my parents' home on Thanksgiving.

2. Many people have parties on New Year's Eve. (New Year's Eve / when)

   _____

3. At the end of the year, Japanese people give and receive *oseibo* presents to show their appreciation for the people in their lives. (exchange)

   _____

4. June is the month when many Brazilians celebrate the Festa Junina. (in June)

   _____

5. In Sweden, people observe Midsummer's Day around June 21. (occur)

   _____

10 **Imagine you are in a foreign country and someone has invited you to a New Year's Eve party. Ask questions about the party using the words in the box or your own ideas.**

| ☐ clothes | ☐ midnight | ☐ sing and dance |
| ☐ fireworks | ☑ present | ☐ special food |

1. _Should I bring a New Year's present?_

2. _____

3. _____

4. _____

5. _____

6. _____